All of Me: Light Work, Heavy History

A Collection of Poetry & Prose

by

Emily Clarida

Copyright

Copyright © 2026 **Emily Clarida**

All rights reserved.

No part of this book may be reproduced, distributed, or transmitted in any form or by any means, electronic, mechanical, photocopying, recording, or otherwise, without the prior written permission of the author, except in the case of brief quotations used in reviews or scholarly works.

Disclaimer

This work is a blend of memory, history, ancestry, and creative interpretation. While rooted in lived experience and familial truth, certain names, timelines, events, and details may be altered or reimagined for literary and artistic purposes.

This book is not intended to serve as a factual historical record, genealogical document, or legal account, but rather as a personal and poetic exploration of identity, inheritance, and healing.

Photo & Ancestral Materials Notice

Photographs included in this work are either original to the author, used with permission, or believed to be in the public domain. Ancestral references, historical records, and genealogical materials are shared for personal, educational, and commemorative purposes.

ISBN Notice

ISBN: 979-8-9994970-6-2

Edition

First Edition

Dedication

For my father,

Howard Clarida (1932–1979),

and for my grandparents,

Louis Mason Clarida

and Emma Elizabeth Stamper Clarida,

whose survival became my inheritance.

Epigraph

We are not broken.

We are layered.

Table of Contents

A Blessing for My Grandchild 1

Ancestral Prelude: What We Built 2
    Loss and the Body 3
    The First Leaving: Ohio 4
    Westward: Palo Alto Before the Name 4
    What They Built 5
    What Reached Me 6
    Closing 6

The Glow: Beauty, Confidence & Femininity 7

Indigo Light 8
    Affirmation for Sharing My Light 8

Lucky 9

Be Soft With Me 11

What the Body Remembers 13
    Affirmation 13
    Reflection 14

Millie Young (1774) 15

Wake Up, Beloved 17

Aurora & the Bird 19

The Weight: Ancestry, Trauma & Mixed Identity 21

For Howard Clarida (1932–1979) 22

Bill of Sale, Bill of Survival 25

What Blood Conceals, a Will Confirms 27

The Blood That Crossed Oceans 30

Every Inch Within Me 31
    Reflection 31
    The Place That Remembered Me 32

Ghana: Where the Ocean Remembers 33
   Reflection 34
   The Land That Carried Me Home 34

Ghana: The Shoreline of Return 36
   Reflection 36
   The Gift of Return...37

When the Voodoo Winds Whisper 38

The River Said, Go East 39

When the Boo Hag Came to Da Nang 40

Between Hoodoo and the Crescent Moon 42

My Ancestors Pray in Two Languages 43

The Rootwoman's Crescent 45

For Great-Aunt Delian.. 47

Fo' Great-Aunt Delian 49

Between Coasts and Kinfolk 50

My Bloodline Wasn't Asked for Permission..................... 52

I Am the Story That Survived 55

Mixed by History, Loved by Me 58

Samuel Manning Stood Up 59

Free Before Freedom...61

The First Daughter of a Promise...................................... 63

Clarissa of the Three Rivers 65

Henry of Gordon County.. 66

Where My Blood Remembers 67

Salt Carried Inland.. 69

Sea Island Made 71

The Fight: Colorism, Stereotypes & Resilience............73

    Lies They Fed Us 74

    We Shine Anyway 76

    Saltwater Reunion 79

    Candle for the Scammer 82

    We Ain't for Sale 84

    Lowcountry Conjure Man 86
        Lowcountry Conjure & Soul Power 87

    Crossfire Queen 90

    Light Skin Don't Mean Light Work 92

    PYT at the Funeral 94

    Graveside Prayer 95

    For Mike 96

    Riding Through Fear 97

    The Man Who Survived the Rivers 99

The Rise: Healing, Pride & Self-Love 101

    STD 102

    The Way I Heal 104

    I Call My Spirit Back from the Boo Hag 106

    Morning Bus Peace 108

    Between the Lines (West Liberty Avenue) 109
        Author's Note 111

The Future: Vision, Empowerment & Joy 112

    We Been One 113

    Royal Remix 115

Both Black & Unbothered 117

A Letter to My First Grandbaby 119

Acknowledgments 120

About the Author 121

Ritual Sound 122

Permissions & Credits 123

Connect with the Author 124

Author's Note

All of Me: Light Work, Heavy History is a reflection on what we carry and what carries us. These poems and prose pieces were written over time, shaped by memory, lineage, love, and loss. Some moments are precise; others are felt rather than remembered. All of them are true in the way truth lives in the body.

This book does not attempt to document history in full, but to explore how history lives within us ~ how it shapes identity, resilience, and the quiet work of becoming whole.

A Blessing for My Grandchild

For the one arriving with new light.

May your spirit remember what your mouth has not yet learned.
May your feet recognize safe ground.
May your name be spoken with tenderness
and corrected with love.

May the ancestors lean in when you laugh
and stand tall when you are afraid.
May your hands learn both softness and strength.
May you know when to stay
and when to go.

May you never doubt that you belong~
to your people,
to your purpose,
to yourself.

You are covered.
You are claimed.
You are already loved.

Ancestral Prelude: What We Built

Some histories arrive fully documented.
Others arrive in fragments ~ names held by family, dates written later, memories carried in the body when paper falls short.

My family's story lives in both places.

What exists is enough to know we were here.
What is missing tells its own truth.

My family's roots stretch through Walker County and Gordon County, Georgia, where Black life in the late 1800s was measured carefully and documented selectively. My grandparents, Louis Mason Clarida and Emma Elizabeth Stamper Clarida, were born into a world where Black existence was recorded when it served labor, inheritance, or control ~ and neglected when it required care.

Their names appear clearly in my great-grandfather's will. Property, kinship, and obligation were recorded with precision. Births, however, were another matter.

In the early twentieth century, many Black children in the South were born at home, attended by midwives whose knowledge sustained families even when the state refused to witness them properly. Birth certificates were often delayed, misfiled, or never created at all. This absence was not accidental. It reflected whose lives were considered worthy of attention.

People existed fully, even when the systems meant to record them chose not to look.

Loss and the Body

Louis Mason Clarida worked when work was available. Survival followed seasons, scarcity, and the fragile economics of the Jim Crow South. By the early 1930s, poverty had begun to register in the body. Pellagra, a disease born of malnutrition and limited access to adequate food, was common among poor Black families whose diets were shaped by necessity, not choice.

People did not talk much about sickness. They endured it.

Loss had already visited the household before Louis's body began to fail. In 1930, Beatrice Clarida, a thirteen-year-old daughter of the family, died. She was still a child, old enough to be known and loved, young enough that her absence would have changed the rhythm of the home. The records do not explain why. Many deaths of poor Black children were never fully written down; illness moved quietly through homes already strained by hunger and limited care. Families learned not to ask too many questions. They learned instead to continue.

Louis died in 1934.

He left behind Emma and their children, including a son barely old enough to understand absence ~ my father, Howard Clarida, just two years old. Loss arrived early, without explanation or ceremony. There was no time for prolonged mourning. Life required movement.

Though Louis died away from his birthplace, he was carried home and buried in Sugar Valley, Gordon County, Georgia, where his people were from. Returning the dead required effort ~ money, coordination, and community. Families did not do this casually. Burial was not only about rest. It was about belonging, about having your name spoken correctly by the land. Beatrice had been returned there four years earlier, the child already resting in the same red Georgia soil that would later receive him.

Louis was laid to rest where his life began.

The First Leaving: Ohio

Emma was left to decide how to go on.

The first to leave was Aunt Mary, the eldest daughter. She married Rudy, who became my uncle by marriage. Rudy was a skilled furrier, raising chinchillas and crafting coats by hand ~ work that required patience, precision, and knowledge passed through practice rather than privilege.

Mary and Rudy moved ahead to Ohio, creating a foothold before the rest of the family followed. Migration did not happen all at once. It rarely does. It moves first through one brave decision, then another.

Once stability existed, Emma followed with the remaining children. Cleveland was not a dream ~ it was a strategy. Proximity to work. Proximity to kin. Proximity to a growing Black community built by others who had already left the South behind.

Migration, in this way, was collective. Survival arranged through family.

Westward: Palo Alto Before the Name

From Ohio, the family moved again ~ this time west. They settled in Palo Alto, California, long before it would be called Silicon Valley, before technology replaced orchards and working neighborhoods, before the land was renamed.

They arrived before the world arrived.

California was not yet a promise. It was distance. Distance from Southern terror. Distance from scarcity. Distance from graves that carried too much history. What they built there was not industry, but continuity ~ children raised with a steadier sense of possibility.

My family did not arrive late to opportunity.
They arrived early to place.

What They Built

Survival did not look the same for everyone.

Uncle Louis, became a preacher, building spiritual shelter where institutions offered none. Aunt Laura ~ also known as Halima, claimed her body as art, becoming a belly dancer and teacher, owning a studio where movement was discipline, expression, and liberation.

Rudy, my uncle by marriage, built an economic life through his work as a furrier ~ raising animals, crafting garments, sustaining household stability in a time when such opportunities were limited.

My father, Howard Clarida, became a builder in the most literal sense. He worked in construction, dynamiting underwater to help build bridges, shaping infrastructure that allowed others to cross safely. He built things meant to last ~ roads, structures, foundations ~ often unseen, always necessary.

I would later understand this as inheritance.

What Reached Me

I was born in October of 1973, into a family that had already crossed states, histories, and losses. My father loved me with presence, playfulness, and protection. He understood that gentleness could be resistance. That safety was something a child should feel without explanation.

When he died, I was young ~ but not untouched. Memory stayed. Longing stayed. Love did not disappear; it settled.

What I carry now is not only grief.
It is continuity.

A family that endured neglect without disappearing.
A lineage that built spiritual, cultural, and physical structures.
A history that survived because people chose to keep moving.

Closing

What I inherited was not ease.
It was endurance shaped into usefulness.
Light carried carefully through heavy years.
History held in the body, then released through work, faith, movement, and love.

My family did not escape history.
They lived through it ~
building what they could, where they were,
until survival became something sturdier than fear.

This is what light work looks like
when history is heavy.

The Glow: Beauty, Confidence & Femininity

This section honors your radiance ~ the softness, power, and feminine brilliance that move with you even when the world cannot name it. These poems celebrate your glow, your intuition, and the beauty you carry effortlessly.

Indigo Light

I was born beneath a whispering sky,
Ancient eyes in a child's face.
The world called me strange ~
but the moon called me home.

I walk between silence and song,
feeling the stories in every stone.
I heal without meaning to,
love without asking,
and glow without trying.

They say I never age ~
perhaps they're right.
For time cannot touch
a soul made of starlight.

Affirmation for Sharing My Light

I speak from my soul, not for approval but for truth.
My stories are sacred threads of who I am ~
woven from ancestors, dreams, and divine memory.
I share only with those who can hold my light gently.
My voice is safe, my spirit is guided,
and my words travel exactly where they're meant to go.

Lucky

He arrived in my life the way
certain people do ~
quiet at first,
like morning light slipping into a room
I didn't know had windows.

There was something golden about him,
a brightness that didn't announce itself,
just glowed.
The kind of presence that makes
ordinary days feel sun-kissed,
even when the sky is undecided.

We crossed paths on a warm coast,
where laughter comes easy
and time moves soft.
Two wanderers who weren't looking
for anything except maybe
a reason to stay a little longer.

For a while, the world felt simple ~
soft nights, shared jokes,
hands brushing like they had secrets
to exchange.
There are some seasons
that feel like music
you didn't know you needed.

But life has a way of stretching distance
between people who once felt close enough
to touch without reaching.
Sometimes hearts don't fall out ~
they just drift
in opposite directions.

Even so, I carry the good ~
the joy,
the light,
the part of me that learned
how to open,
how to feel,
how to risk tenderness again.

Some people are storms.
Some are lessons.
But every now and then,
if you're lucky,
someone comes along
and reminds you
you're still capable
of love.

Be Soft With Me

I have to stop swinging on myself
every time I fall short.
Stop acting like I'm supposed to be perfect
when I know damn well
I'm still healing from things
nobody ever apologized for.

I need to learn to talk nice to myself ~
the same way I speak life into others,
the same way I hold space
for folks who don't always hold space for me.

Because I keep expecting me from people ~
expecting my loyalty,
my depth,
my way of loving and showing up.
But they ain't me.
And that's where I get cut every time.

Truth is, I've been disappointed by others…
but the biggest heartbreak
is how many times
I've stood in my own way.
How I looked in the mirror
and demanded a version of myself
that wasn't ready yet.

So I'm practicing grace now.
Practicing softness.
Practicing letting myself be human
without a punishment attached.

I'm learning to slow my breathing,
unclench my jaw,
and stop calling myself weak

for needing a little tenderness.

I'm learning that being gentle with myself
isn't letting myself off the hook ~
it's showing up for the girl inside me
who kept surviving
even when I tried to rush her healing.

This is my promise:
I will not be my own bully anymore.
I will not strip myself of joy
just because someone else mishandled me.

I will love me
like I expect to be loved ~
fully, honestly,
and without conditions.

What the Body Remembers

There is a mark where I carry,
low and quiet,
where stories settle before they are spoken.
It is not loud.
It does not beg to be seen.
It simply remembers.

Another mark rests on my knee,
where movement begins again.
Where bending does not mean breaking.
Where rising has become a language
my body speaks fluently.

One holds.
One walks.

Together they say
I was never meant to collapse
under what I carry.
I was built to bring it forward~
softly, steadily,
with my whole self intact.

Affirmation

I honor the wisdom written on my body.
I trust what I carry and how I move through the world.
I am strong enough to hold truth
and gentle enough to walk it forward.
My body remembers resilience,
and I move in alignment with my purpose.
What I carry becomes legacy, not burden.

Reflection

Reading the Marks with Compassion

When I look at my body, I no longer ask what is wrong.
I ask what it has survived.
What it has carried without complaint.
What it has learned how to move forward.
The marks on my skin are not interruptions.
They are punctuation~
pauses that remind me to listen.
They tell me that holding and moving can coexist.
That strength does not always roar.
That legacy is often quiet,
walking itself into the future one step at a time.
I am allowed to honor my body
as a witness,
a keeper,
and a guide.

Millie Young (1774)

She was born
before freedom learned how to speak plainly.
Before liberty was anything
but a rumor moving through trees.

South Carolina held its breath
the year she arrived~
earth unsettled,
names shifting,
truth written louder than it was lived.

By the time she could walk,
the world was splitting itself in two.
Men called it a revolution.
Women called it keeping children alive.

Millie learned early
that history is not something you watch~
it passes through you.
In the sound of cannons.
In the tightening of hands.
In the quiet discipline of endurance.

No record tells us
what she believed,
who she trusted,
what prayers she learned by heart.
Only that she remained.

That she grew
inside uncertainty,
inside a nation inventing itself
without asking the women
who held it together.

I carry her now~
not as legend,
but as labor.
As breath.
As proof that survival
is its own form of light.

Millie Young,
born into upheaval,
ancestor of becoming,
your history was heavy~
and still,
you endured long enough
to become mine.

Millie Young was a Black woman born in 1774 in South Carolina. Her early life unfolded during the American Revolutionary period, in a colony where Black people~enslaved and free~lived under constant threat, displacement, and erasure. While the nation claimed independence, Black women like Millie carried the weight of survival without recognition, their lives preserved more through lineage than record.

Wake Up, Beloved

We are the children of sun and soil,
the echo of drumbeats that teach hearts to rise.
We carved kingdoms from shadows,
built futures from ashes ~
and still, they try to convince us
we are less than our ancestors' dreams.

Wake up.

Our blood remembers greatness
even when our minds forget.
We are the first language,
the original rhythm,
a genius misunderstood
because we keep dimming our brilliance
to make others comfortable.

Wake up.

Stop letting the world define us
by our wounds instead of our wonders.
Stop believing the lie
that we must imitate anyone
just to be worthy.

Loving Black is not a slogan ~
it is protection,
it is restoration,
it is choosing survival
and calling it joy.

Our men are not disposable.
Our women are not burdens.
Our children are not problems ~
they are prophecies

waiting to be believed.

Wake up.

We are not each other's competition.
We are kin.
We are community.
We are the answer our ancestors whispered
into the bones of the earth.

Fix each other's crowns.
Feed each other's dreams.
Teach what was stolen.
Rebuild what was broken.
Honor what was holy
before they renamed it.

Wake up, beloved ~
not to fight each other
but to fight for each other.

Because the most radical revolution
is to love Black people
fiercely, loudly, and forever ~
starting with the reflection
God gifted you in the mirror.

Wake up.
We're not done rising yet.

Aurora & the Bird

I stood beside Aurora,
palm on her bark,
waiting for the bus
and unwinding the day
one breath at a time.

Then a great bird swept over me ~
huge wings cutting the sky,
majestic enough to bless me,
sudden enough to shake me.

And every fear I carry
rose up at once:
the fast-running bugs,
the creatures that leap or fly,
even the two-legged beings
whose shadows stretch long.
Everything that moves
has startled me at some point,
taught my body to brace
before my mind can speak.

But Aurora stayed still.
Rooted.
Patient.
Letting my fingers find calm
in the grooves of her skin.
A reminder
that not everything towering above me
is meant to harm me.
Some things simply move
because that is their nature.

Maybe fear is just the echo
of moments I survived.

Maybe the bird was not a warning,
but a mirror ~
showing me how big things
don't have to break me,
how sudden shadows
don't have to send me running.

So I stood there
with Aurora grounding my hand,
the bird disappearing into the dusk,
and me learning, slowly,
to let the world move
without shrinking from it.

Because even fear
can be a teacher.
And even I
am learning to stay.

The Weight: Ancestry, Trauma & Mixed Identity

This section carries the weight of origin ~ the oceans crossed, the bloodlines whispered, and the stories that shaped identity before language could. These poems trace memory across continents, honoring the beauty and ache of belonging to many worlds at once.

For Howard Clarida (1932–1979)

My father was gentle
in a world that was not.

He carried joy like a quiet rebellion,
like a soft answer to a hard life
he never fully explained to me,
but lived through anyway.

He took me for ice cream cones
stacked taller than my small hands,
laughed while it melted down my wrists,
as if sweetness should always overflow.

He took me to feed the ducks ~
and when one bit my lip,
he lost his mind on that duck,
protective fury wrapped in love,
as if nothing on this earth
had the right to hurt me.

He laid on the floor with me,
watched Sesame Street and Mr. Rogers,
let the world slow down
until it fit my size.

He built my Lincoln Logs with care,
knowing I would knock them down,
and never once asked me
to stop being destructive in play,
because he understood
that creation and ruin
are both ways children learn power.

He spoiled me.
Not with things ~ but with attention.

With presence.
With the feeling that I mattered
simply because I existed.

When I became obsessed with crutches
and wheelchairs ~
strange little curiosities of motion and stillness ~
he didn't shame me.
He asked strangers to let me look closer,
let me touch the mystery of survival,
long before I knew
how much survival lived inside him too.

He took me to my grandmother's house
for Brach's peppermints,
and laughed while she ~ old and fierce ~
got down on the floor with me,
telling me to fight,
to put the karate on her,
as if strength should be learned early
and joy should always be loud.

I was young.
Too young to know
how much time costs.

Too young to understand
that love like this
is not promised to last long ~
only to last deep.

When he died,
he did not leave me empty.
He left me full of memory,
so full that grief had somewhere to live.

I carry him in small habits:
in my tenderness,
in my rage when someone hurts what I love,
in my longing for what felt safe and true.

He was my heart.
Still is.

And even now,
decades later,
I know this much to be sacred:

Some fathers don't disappear.
They become the ground
their children stand on.

Bill of Sale, Bill of Survival

On my wall hangs a paper
inked in another man's power ~
a receipt for a life
measured in dollars and debt.

Seventeen years old,
my ancestor Ned
stood on soil that called itself free,
but shackled his breath anyway.

Four hundred forty dollars ~
the price of his heartbeat,
the value they wrote
for a boy becoming a man
in chains.

But I am here ~
his 2nd great-granddaughter,
rooted in his refusal
to disappear.

I touch the frame gently,
not to honor the sale ~
but the survival,
the miles of memory
that brought me here.

For every great-grandmother
born under bondage,
for every grandfather
counted like cattle,
I rise.

Ned's blood ~
unbought, unbroken ~

runs in my veins
like a freedom he never saw
but dreamed into me.

I carry his name
into rooms he couldn't enter,
into futures he was denied,
into joy he never tasted.

They sold his body ~
but not his becoming.
I am the proof
of his price
and his pricelessness.

Every day I look at that bill of sale
and whisper to the boy who lived:

Thank you, Ned.
Your freedom found me.

What Blood Conceals, a Will Confirms

On paper,
they called him Master.
But the will he wrote
spoke a different kind of truth:

Jerry Moore ~ to be freed.
Viney ~ to be freed.
Their children ~ to be freed.
Not sold.
Not divided.
Not erased.

Instead ~
silver, horses, cattle, furniture,
the chest and the kettle
passed from his house to theirs.
Gifts a man does not leave
to people he claims are nothing.

So we read the lines between the lines:
these were his children too.

Viney ~ born in bondage,
yet protected in ink,
likely carved from the same blood
that tried to own her.

Jerry ~ thirty years strong,
once given a price,
then given a future.

Their babies named,
not tallied.
Their marriage honored,
not forbidden.

Their freedom ordered
by the very hand
that once claimed their breath.

This truth is sharp
and soft
all at once.

To be your father's property
and
your father's child ~
a wound and a witness.

But Jerry and Viney
took what was owed
and built what was theirs.

They left that plantation
not empty-handed ~
but carrying proof of survival:
a copper kettle,
documents declaring ownership
of themselves.

And generation after generation,
we survived that contradiction.

I speak their names boldly now:
Elvira "Viney" Moore.
Jeremiah "Jerry" Moore.

Born into bondage.
Freed by blood.
Remembered by me.

I am their descendant ~

made of what was done in secret
and what was written for the record.

What blood concealed,
a will confirmed.
And I rise
because they did.

The Blood That Crossed Oceans

My blood is a map,
written in tides and moonlight.
Nigeria hums in my heartbeat,
Sierra Leone braids my dreams,
and somewhere between the Ganges and the Gulf of Siam,
a grandmother hums a song I've never learned ~
but somehow know.

Twelve generations whisper my name
through rice fields and red earth,
through temples carved with prayer
and coasts that remember the trade winds.
They crossed oceans without ships,
leaving memory folded in my bones.

When I walked through Cham ruins,
the wind knew me ~
called me "child of the in-between,"
a daughter of roads unmarked by borders.
And I wept,
not from sadness,
but from recognition.

My lineage is not a straight line ~
it's a constellation.
Each point a story,
each story a heartbeat,
each heartbeat
a homecoming.

Every Inch Within Me

Sometimes I hesitate to mention those tiny percentages ~
the fragments, the 1% or 2%, the whispers in my DNA.
They seem so small, almost invisible on paper.
But to me, they are galaxies.

Each trace is a story that survived.
A spark that crossed an ocean,
a name that might have been forgotten,
a song that somehow still hums in my bones.

I used to think the small numbers didn't matter ~
but now I see that they are the threads,
the sacred dust that ties me
to every shore my ancestors ever touched.

Even a drop of water carries
the memory of the mountain it came from.
And I, too, carry every river, every land, every voice ~
every inch within me.

Reflection

I've learned that ancestry isn't about how much, but how *deeply* something lives within you. The smallest fragments often hold the greatest truths ~ because they are what remain after centuries of movement, survival, and transformation.

When I look at those small numbers on my DNA test, I don't see statistics. I see doors. Each one opens to a place, a people, a memory that somehow found its way into me. It's humbling ~ to realize how vast the story of one person can be.

So I no longer measure myself by percentages. I measure by the heartbeat I feel when I stand in a place that feels like home, even when I've never been there before. That's the real inheritance ~ not numbers, but remembrance.

The Place That Remembered Me

Vietnam has a way of speaking without words.
The air feels older here ~ like it remembers. When I walk through the Cham ruins or stand by the sea, I feel something beneath the surface of time. It isn't imagination. It's remembrance.

Even though this land wasn't listed by name on my DNA chart, my spirit recognized it before my eyes did. The wind feels familiar, the colors of the earth stir something ancient inside me. I understand now ~ my ancestors didn't only leave me blood; they left me *direction*.

Maybe they passed through here generations ago. Maybe they simply left their blessings in the soil. Either way, I am not a stranger.
I am a return.

And in this place ~ between memory and belonging ~ I am learning that home isn't always where you begin.
Sometimes, it's where the land whispers back,
"I remember you, too."

Ghana: Where the Ocean Remembers

I came to Ghana twice ~
once for family,
once for love.

The first time, I stood in Teshie Nungua,
where my cousin lives ~
the great-granddaughter of Uncle Garfield,
my grandfather's brother
who once called this coastline home.
The sea there didn't speak,
it *sang*.
And in its rhythm, I heard the pulse of homecoming.

The second time,
I returned for a man from Port Harcourt ~
an Igbo heart wrapped in laughter and distance.
He took me to the slave castles
where walls breathe history
and the air still carries the prayers
of those who left but never truly left.

In Osu, I learned how the night can feel alive.
In Weija, how silence can hold a name.
And in every place,
Ghana held me ~
not as a guest,
but as someone the land already knew.

Two visits, two kinds of love:
one bound by blood,
one by longing.
Both reminding me
that the ocean remembers
what we think we've forgotten.

Reflection

Ghana was more than a trip ~ it was a reunion.
Every shoreline, every market, every sound of drums told me that my story didn't start in America; it began in the heartbeat of Africa.

To visit family in Teshie Nungua was to meet living history ~ a continuation of what my grandfather's generation had carried across time. And to return later for love was to learn that the same ocean that once separated us could also bring connection.

Standing in those castles ~ Cape Coast, Elmina, and the quiet ruins that still smell of salt and sorrow ~ I felt both pain and peace. Pain for what was taken. Peace for what survived. Because *I am what survived.*

Ghana reminded me that love, family, and ancestry are not separate stories. They are waves of the same sea ~ always returning to shore.

The Land That Carried Me Home

Ghana felt like a mirror held up to my soul.
Every breeze that passed through Osu, every wave that touched the shore at Weija, whispered, *"You've been here before."* I didn't have to search for belonging ~ the land offered it freely, as if it had been waiting for me to remember.

In Teshie Nungua, my cousin's laughter felt like a bridge between past and present ~ proof that what was once separated had found its way back together. And in those stone castles, where the ocean speaks in grief and grace, I touched the walls and felt both loss and strength. The air was heavy, but it didn't crush me. It carried me.

I came to Ghana for family and for love, but I left with
something greater ~ a sense of continuity.
A truth that home isn't only the place where you are born,
but the place that holds your story when you return.

In Ghana, I met my ancestors not as ghosts,
but as echoes that still walk beside me.
And as I left its shores, I realized ~
the land didn't say goodbye.
It said, *"Welcome back."*

Ghana: The Shoreline of Return

Ghana stands between memory and the sea,
where waves carry whispers from centuries past.
Stone walls still breathe the weight of history,
and the ocean moves as if it remembers every name.

Here, the air hums with the rhythm of drums
that once called children home at dusk
and now call descendants back across time.

The earth in Teshie Nungua feels alive beneath the feet ~
soft with stories, firm with survival.
In Osu, night falls with laughter and music.
In Weija, dawn rises in quiet reflection.

This land holds no strangers.
It welcomes those who listen.
And those who listen
find that home is not a place you seek ~
it is a place that waits for you to remember.

Reflection

For many in the diaspora, Ghana is more than a nation ~ it is a threshold.
It stands as both a beginning and a return, a place where history breathes through ocean air and stone. The castles along the coast are not only reminders of loss, but monuments of endurance ~ proof that the spirit cannot be contained by walls or chains.

When one walks these shores, it is not as a visitor but as a descendant retracing steps once taken in sorrow, now in remembrance. Ghana offers what few places can: a space to reconcile past and present, to grieve and to heal, to touch the soil and know ~ *we are still here.*

The Gift of Return

Ghana gives more than history ~ it gives peace.
Not the kind found in silence, but the kind that rises from knowing you have come full circle. The land doesn't ask for proof of belonging; it recognizes your presence, as if to say, *"We never forgot you."*

In the rhythm of the waves and the warmth of the people, there is restoration. The heaviness of memory softens into gratitude. The air itself feels like a blessing ~ an embrace from the past that says, *"You are part of the story still."*

To walk here is to stand at the edge of remembrance and renewal.
It is to understand that what was taken was not destroyed, and what survives within us ~ the courage, the song, the faith ~

is the true return.

When the Voodoo Winds Whisper

When dusk embraced your voice,
and breath became deep velvet,
you summoned spirits in song ~
you wove prophecy in chord and pulse.

Michael, you danced between shadows
and light, with that raspy hush
that trembled like ancient souls
calling home across time.

Your **Voodoo** was more than music ~
a bridge between blood and song,
a prayer in bass and breath
that honored our ancestors' whispers.

Tonight the sky holds its breath,
the moon tilts a little lower;
your voice drifts in the smoke of memory,
singing to those who still listen.

I carry you in my marrow ~
every note, a drum in my heart,
inspired by roots deep as earth,
by your courage in silence and sound.

Rest now, spirit of song,
your name etched in eternity,
and when the wind hums low,
I'll hear you ~
D'Angelo ~
ever alive in pulse and promise.

The River Said, Go East

The river called your name, child ~
not in English,
not in Gullah tongue,
but in the hum of palm leaves and prayer bells.

We been followin' you 'cross oceans,
watchin' you remember who you was
before they told you who to be.

Vietnam ain't strange ground ~
it's soil that knows your heartbeat,
same rhythm that fed rice and okra,
same sun that kissed your kin in Carolina fields.

You think you travelin',
but it's us walkin' you home,
one temple step, one incense breath,
one ancestor dream at a time.

We lead you where the water is calm,
where the spirits don't shout,
they whisper ~
and if you listen soft enough,
you'll hear your own voice
callin' you back to your beginning.

When the Boo Hag Came to Da Nang

for my 52nd birthday

She came back riding the monsoon wind,
crossing waters older than memory.
Not Charleston this time ~
but Da Nang, where I came to rest,
to eat, to laugh, to make something new.
Yet she found me,
that witch who remembers my breath.

My legs were drumming the floorboards,
my voice a torn ribbon of sound.
She sat on my chest, heavy as history,
pressing sleep into stone.
I wanted to say her name,
but my tongue was caught in both oceans.

Are you my Geechee kin,
salt rising from rice fields and low-country mud?
Or a Southeast shadow ~
a spirit who knows I carry too many ancestors
to sleep clean through the night?

You've been here before,
hotel room in Charleston,
humid and humming with ghosts.
You whispered: *come with me.*
And I remembered my grandmother's warning ~
talk if you must, but never take her hand.

So I wake, trembling, older again,
half grateful, half undone.
What are you teaching me this time?
That I cannot outrun the stories in my blood?
That every birthday is a crossroads

where the living and the gone exchange gifts ~
mine: fear and fire,
yours: a reminder that I'm still chosen
to walk between worlds.

Between Hoodoo and the Crescent Moon

I carry two rivers in my bones ~
one born of rootwork,
one born of Qur'anic breath.
Both crossed the Atlantic
inside the hearts of my people.

The Fulani whispered prayers into leather
and tied them against the storm.
The Mende called on the spirits of iron and rain.
And somewhere in the hold of that dark ship,
Hoodoo and Islam touched hands
and promised to keep us alive.

So I walk with a Bible psalm in my left palm,
and an ancestor's amulet warming my right.
I pray in the rhythm of my grandmother's humming,
and bow in the direction
my great-grandmothers once faced the dawn.

I am the child of rootwomen and moon-watchers,
of conjure smoke and desert wind.
A woman standing at the crossroads ~
not divided,
but doubled.

Everything they carried,
carries me.

My Ancestors Pray in Two Languages

My spirit was braided long before I was born ~
Fulani on the wind,
Mende in the water,
Gullah Geechee in the earth beneath my feet.

I come from women who healed with Psalm and plant,
who called on spirits
and still remembered the rhythm of the crescent moon.
From men who hid prayers in their hands,
folded like amulets against the whip.

Some ancestors wrote their power ~
Arabic curling like smoke,
African symbols shining like breath.
Some spoke their medicine ~
Bible verses soft as balm,
herbs crushed between steady palms.

And in me,
their languages rise like twin flames.

I am the grandchild of conjure and Qur'an,
of storm-born daughters
and sunrise-seeking sons.
Their footsteps echo in my marrow,
their faiths sit together in my chest
like old friends who always knew
they shared the same story.

Call me contradiction ~
I am not.
I am inheritance.
I am memory made flesh.
I am the bridge they built to survive.

When I pray,
the ancestors lean in close ~
some humming the Psalms,
others whispering Bismillah ~
all of them blessing me
in the languages they carried
so I could walk whole.

The Rootwoman's Crescent

I was raised by women who knew the salt of the tide
and the salt of a prayer.
Women who carried iron in their pockets,
Psalms on their tongues,
and Africa in their eyes.

They stepped gentle,
but their shadows were long ~
rootwomen who could read a storm
before the sky even darkened.

My great-grandmothers stitched power into fabric,
hid blessings in seams,
and whispered words so old
they tasted like river clay and moonlight.

Some of them prayed with beads,
rolling ancient syllables like honey in the mouth.
Some prayed with roots,
burning cedar and sweetgrass
till the room glowed gold.

But all of them ~
every single one ~
walked with a crescent moon tucked behind the heart
and a Bible verse tucked beneath the breast.

And I ~
child of Fulani dawn,
granddaughter of Mende night,
Geechee woman standing in the doorway of worlds ~
I am the one who remembers.

I call their names
and the air grows thick.

I pour the libation
and the floorboards hum.
I say the prayer
and the whole house shifts,
as if the ancestors leaned forward
to hear me better.

I am their bridge,
their prophecy,
their returning.

Between root and revelation,
between Hoodoo and the crescent moon,
I walk whole,
blessed,
and chosen ~
same as they were.

For Great-Aunt Delian

You were here
only once on paper ~
June girl
age eight
in the Joseys sun,
a name pressed softly
into the census
like a flower
between fragile pages.

The world wrote you down
and then misplaced you ~
a whisper in the ledger,
a footstep in red Georgia clay,
a giggle lost
to the pine trees
and the wind.

But blood remembers
what ink forgets.
Your mother's hands
carried your laughter
into every child she held
after you.
Your sisters' eyes
still mirror your light.
Your nieces and nephews
walk with your tenderness
in their bones.

No stone marks the place
your small dreams slept,
but your memory
restores its own ground ~
right here

in the heart of those who call you
kin.

Great-Aunt Delian,
we gather you back
from the silence.
We speak your name
so the ancestors
know you stood among them.

You were loved.
You are loved still.

Rest, little one ~
your story is home again.

Fo' Great-Aunt Delian

Chile, you name bin whisper
'cross dat Josey breeze,
June chile, barefoot laughin'
'round de pine-tree leaves.

Dey write you once on paper,
den de ink gone dry,
but de blood ain' forget, nah ~
it remember why.

You mama heart cry silent,
but she keep you near,
carry you in de prayers
she hum fo' all she chile here.

Ain' no stone call you by name,
ain' no marker show,
but you spirit walk wid we ~
dat how family grow.

We call you back fo' de elders,
tell um who you be:
Delian ~ sweet lil' gal
dat set we people free.

You bin loved den,
you loved now,
dat love ain' fade or roam.
Rest easy, lil' auntie ~
you story come back home.

Between Coasts and Kinfolk

I've loved men whose roots
drink from rivers I've never crossed ~
men who call islands home,
men who speak to ancestors
in languages my tongue can't always trace.

We share skin like a passport.
Melanin like a flag.
But our histories…
they don't always shake hands.

He says, "We are all the same,"
while I carry a lineage
that built the bones of this country ~
a culture so foundational
they pretend they can't see it.

My people's songs are in the soil.
Our fingerprints are in the Capitol bricks,
the cotton fields,
the kitchen tables,
the church pews
that taught us how to resurrect joy
after every crucifixion.

Yet some look at me
like I slipped through a crack in the ocean ~
like I washed up without a tribe,
without a language,
without a name.

They forget we forged all three
right here.

I'm trying to love Pan-African,

but Pan-African don't always love me back.
Not when his pride builds walls
against the story I come from.

So I want a love
that understands my grandmother's hands.
A love that knows why my soul
sounds like a Sunday choir.
A love that honors the ghosts
who built this land
and never got thanked for it.

If he wants my heart,
he must know the map inside it:
Southern dirt,
Gullah breath,
ring shouts rising from the shore.

I am not missing culture.
I am culture that America wears
like its favorite skin.

If he cannot respect the soil I come from ~
then he cannot harvest love here.

My Bloodline Wasn't Asked for Permission

I have loved men
from rivers and islands
where drums still remember their names ~
Yoruba hearts, Igbo smiles,
Garifuna fire,
Belizean warmth in their hands.

They treated me well.
They held me soft.
But they did not know me.

They did not know
the language of my grandmother's silence,
or the way my body remembers
a country built on my people's bones.

They could not read
the history etched in my cheekbones ~
light as a compromise,
light as a consequence,
light as someone else's choice
forced into my family tree
before consent was ever a word.

I am the granddaughter
of forbidden love
or hidden violence ~
no record of whether it was sweetness
or survival
that mixed my blood
under colonial moons.

I carry a confusion
that was never mine to choose ~
planted in my lineage like a secret

nobody wanted to explain.

So yes, I can love across oceans.
Yes, I can dance with many flags.
Yes, my heart recognizes Blackness
in all its accents.

But I need a love
that knows the ghosts
I sleep beside.

A love that sees
I am Foundational Black American ~
not an orphan of Africa,
not a tourist in my own skin,
not a blank space
between two continents.

I am the daughter
of those who survived here
when "here" tried to kill them.
I am the child
of a land that fed on my people,
yet could not break them.

My ancestors didn't travel to America ~
America grew around them.

So if he wants to love me,
he must love the unanswered questions
in my DNA ~
the joy we resurrected
out of sorrow,
the culture we made
out of ashes.

He must understand
that my roots are complicated ~
but they are **mine**.

And they are sacred.

I Am the Story That Survived

My blood has chapters
no historian can fully trace ~
pages written in stolen tongues,
names scattered like seeds
across oceans that swallowed the proof.

I carry questions
no ancestor had the time
or freedom
to answer.

But do not mistake my mystery
for a missing origin.

I come from the ones
who refused to disappear ~
the builders with no blueprint,
the dreamers with chains on their wrists,
the mothers who birthed tomorrow
behind closed doors
and covered history with quilts.

Yes, I date men
whose ancestors kept their tribes
like treasured last names ~
Yoruba, Igbo, Garifuna,
crests still carved
into family memory.

They look at me
as if I am only America's shadow,
a woman without a homeland.

But I am the architect
of America's soul.

The heartbeat in its music.
The seasoning in its food.
The rhythm in its language.
The courage in its flag.

I am a daughter
of the Foundational.
Of the survivors.
Of the first citizens
who were never invited ~
yet essential.

Light skin not by choice,
but by history.
By secrets.
By forbidden moments
written in candlelight
and erased by morning.

My identity is not confusion.
It is **proof**
that my ancestors endured
what others could not imagine.

I am the story
that made it
through fire.

So I no longer ask,
"Where do I come from?"

I ask,
"Where am I going?"

Because I am not lost ~
I am guided.

Every heartbeat,
a drum.
Every step,
a prophecy.

My ancestors walk with me ~
unseen,
but undeniable ~
whispering:

**"We did not survive
just for you to question
your right to exist."**

Mixed by History, Loved by Me

I didn't pick this face,
this shade,
this story written
before I was born.

I'm mixed with
what they hid
and what survived anyway ~
with secrets and strength,
with "forbidden" love
or unfinished pain.

But I refuse to carry shame
for a past I didn't choose.

I am not confusion ~
I am creation.
I am proof that my people
would not break.

So here I stand,
laughing at the irony ~
complexion kissed by history,
confidence unbothered.

Self-love is my inheritance.
Respect is my birthright.

They tried to erase my identity…
Instead, they made me unforgettable.

Samuel Manning Stood Up

Born in bondage
in the red clay of South Carolina,
year 1816 ~
when freedom was a rumor
that only the wind could carry.

Samuel Manning
learned to work before he learned to dream.
Chains trained his hands,
but not his heartbeat.

He became a father
before the nation dared to call him a man ~
Abram, William, Caroline,
Emma, Mary, Georgia, Elisebeth ~
love born into a world
that tried to own every birth.

But when the war came,
he stood up with the brave:
United States Colored Troops ~ 1864.
Not for medals or monuments,
but so a generation unborn
would never kneel as he did.

He carried a rifle
like a promise ~
that his children would inherit mornings
without overseers.

After the war,
Walker County, Georgia learned his name
not as possession
but as citizen.

He lived long enough
to see himself counted
not as three-fifths
but as whole ~
husband, father, voter,
man.

He died in West Armuchee,
on land not owned by other men,
his story rooted so deep
that even the soil remembers him.

I rise because he stood.
I speak because he survived.
I am free
because Samuel Manning
once looked at America
and chose to fight
for the future
that became me.

Free Before Freedom

Born about 1824,
in Maryland soil that knew the weight of chains ~
but he did not wear them.

John Wesley Maloney was counted free
before freedom had a name in this country.
A Black man choosing his own steps
in a world that wanted to erase the path.

By 1850,
the census wrote what many men feared to say:
"Free."
A word dangerous enough to cost a life,
brave enough to build one.

He stood in Easton
as his own man ~
marrying love,
making a home with Hannah Harriet Barnes,
welcoming children into a future
he intended to change.

Then war arrived,
and he could have stayed home ~
his papers already proved his status.
But John Wesley Maloney
did not measure freedom selfishly.

United States Colored Troops ~
he enlisted in 1863,
rifle in hand,
heart on fire for every soul
still sold beneath the flag.

He fought

so no one would question
the right of his children
to walk into daylight unbent.

When history tries to forget
who the heroes were,
remember this:

My 3rd great-grandfather
was free before the law declared it.
He lived as freedom
before freedom was written.

And because he did,
I do too.

The First Daughter of a Promise

She is the first daughter of a promise
this country never planned to keep.
She breathes in a land
that branded her body
before it ever learned her name.

Her womb remembers
the auction block,
yet still grows gardens.
Her bones remember
the chain,
yet still dance.
Her heart remembers
the loss,
yet still loves.

Freedom was whispered to her
in broken English and Bible verses,
but the soil beneath her feet
still holds the iron.
False freedom tastes like
looking over shoulder,
like "it could be taken back,"
like a mask she must remove
each night to breathe.

She holds the trauma
of women she has never met ~
mothers who labored under sun and sorrow,
who could not keep their children
or their own last names,
yet still prayed for a future
where one Black girl might rise
without apology.

And here she stands ~
the answer to those prayers,
the survival of those screams.

Some days she is soft,
some days she is steel.
Both are holy.
Both are earned.

She carries the weight
of every ancestor's unfinished healing,
but today ~
she begins with herself.

She learns love
not as a weapon
or a bargain
or a performance ~
but as her birthright.

She looks in the mirror
and sees not just one woman,
but a nation of grandmothers
finally exhaling.

Her joy is rebellion.
Her rest is revolution.
Her life is reparations
paid in breath and brilliance.

She is still becoming ~
and that becoming
is a freedom
no one can falsify.

Clarissa of the Three Rivers

Born where the rivers braid steel and sky,
Pittsburgh morning, May winds rising ~
a girl already carrying history in her bones.

Monongahela whispered your name,
as brothers and sisters sprouted like roots
in Pennsylvania soil made stubborn by hope.

You loved, you birthed, you buried, you rose ~
two husbands gone before your own gray years
but you still stitched life together
in ward after ward, house after house,
raising children into futures you'd never see.

You walked city streets when freedom
was still learning to breathe in America,
yet you lived long ~ ninety years strong ~
breathing anyway.

From enslaved footsteps behind you
to grandchildren ahead carving new roads,
you were the quiet bridge
between sorrow and city light.

Clarissa, your name is a lantern now.
We hold it high, so every ancestor
who crossed water and border to reach you
shines through us still.

Henry of Gordon County

Georgia heat baptized you into this world ~
1841, before freedom had a name
your tongue could safely speak.

You became a father young,
your children rising like crops
from red clay and prayers ~
Jefferson, Almedia, Ellard,
Sandal, George, Ada, Mary,
Joshuah, Rosa, Charlie ~
a whole legacy walking.

You worked, you survived,
you signed your name
among the newly qualified voters
determined to be counted
after the war tried to erase men like you.

Your steps crossed county lines ~
Sugar Valley to Chattanooga,
then home again ~
never running, always returning
to the soil that raised you.

Ninety-five winters you saw ~
long enough to watch
your children become ancestors too,
long enough to prove that endurance
is its own kind of victory.

Henry, we carry your name
like a steady flame:
proof that our people
did not simply exist ~
they lived, they loved, they stayed.

Where My Blood Remembers

I am born of rivers crossing oceans,
of kingdoms and coastlines
stitched into my bones.

From Nigeria, where drums first spoke
my heartbeat into existence ~
and Ivory Coast & Ghana,
where gold dust and warrior queens
taught my spirit how to shine.

From Benin & Togo,
where ancestors carved stories into wood
and called lightning by name.

From Mali, empire of scholars
who measured stars before borders existed ~
and Senegal, where voices rise like saltwind,
singing freedom into the sea.

I am Cameroon thunder,
Western Bantu survival ~
a language of strength
carried across the Atlantic in silence
but never erased.

I am footsteps in Alabama red clay,
Georgia pine,
Mississippi river mud ~
Southern soil soaked in faith and rebellion
where cotton fields once whispered
"Live anyway."

But I am also winds from far-off shores:
Scotland's highlands, Welsh hills,
Ireland's rain-soaked green,

France, The Netherlands, England ~
threads woven through history's upheaval
into the tapestry that is me.

I am the coastal plain,
the Piedmont rise,
the journey north to D.C.
when freedom called louder
than fear could silence.

I am all of them ~
every tribe, every tide, every turning.
My DNA is a compass pointing
home in every direction.

Where my ancestors scattered,
my soul gathers ~
and in me, they return
whole.

Salt Carried Inland

(Gullah Geechee from Coast to Capital)

My story starts where water speaks Gullah ~
where the tides teach memory
and rice fields hold the names
of those who would not break.

But my people didn't just stay coastal ~
they carried that salt inland.

Into the Georgia Piedmont,
feet dusty with red clay rebellion,
still hearing the ocean
inside their pulse.

Into Alabama heat,
where hands that once shaped rice
now built futures out of iron and sweat,
singing the same praise-house songs
just louder.

Up through Virginia rivers,
following Underground whispers
like stars stitched into night ~
freedom always a direction,
never a question.

Maryland marshlands caught our breath,
but not our faith ~
we crossed the Lower Mississippi
with the same courage
that crossed the Atlantic.

Back to the Georgia Coastal Plain,
to Jefferson County kin ~

land where Geechee tongues
refused to bow
and grandmothers kept spirits fed
with okra and hymns.

Then north again ~
West Virginia hills on one side,
Northern Virginia light on the other ~
every step a testimony
to what refuses to be erased.

Until finally ~
Washington, D.C.,
where the descendants of the enslaved
stood in the capital
of the enslavers
and said:
We are still here.

I am Gullah Geechee
even off the coast ~
because salt lives in my blood,
tide lives in my walk,
and Africa lives in my tongue
no matter where I rise.

My roots are water.
My branches are everywhere.

Sea Island Made

I am not guessed at.
Not assumed.
Not claimed without receipts.

I am Sea Island made ~
born from the salt
that would not surrender.

My DNA got Savannah
written all through it ~
riverwater and revolution
in the same breath.

My blood hit Brunswick
like a drum ~
Sapelo wind in its lungs,
rice field memory
woven into its spine.

And Jacksonville?
That's just Geechee on the move ~
the coast stretching inland,
roots refusing to stay still
just because freedom called from a distance.

I am the child of tidal people ~
those who braided Africa
into English until the language remembered
who birthed it.

Those who cooked resistance
into pots of red rice and okra stew ~
seasoned with tradition,
served with spirit.

Those who kept their dead
close enough to hear,
but holy enough to honor ~
because nobody crosses over
without still holding the family line.

I walk with the sea behind me
and ancestors ahead ~
I move like the ocean:
unowned, unbroken,
unapologetically alive.

Call me Gullah Geechee ~
not because a test says maybe,
but because my people planted themselves
where the water meets the world
and survived.

Salt still shines in my veins.
The islands still speak my name.
And every step I take
carries the coast with it ~

I am Sea Island Made.

The Fight: Colorism, Stereotypes & Resilience

This section holds the battles you never asked to fight ~ the colorism, the staring eyes, the whispers, the misunderstandings, the stereotypes, and the storms you walked through anyway. Here is where your resilience sharpens, where you refuse erasure, and where you reclaim every inch of your identity.

Lies They Fed Us

They told them I was lazy.
They told me they were arrogant.
They said I was loud.
They said they were rude.
They called us two wrongs
and swore white supremacy was the only right.

They fed them images
of me with chains still invisible,
painted me criminal
before they ever saw my smile.

They fed me stories
of them bowing under crowns not theirs,
painted them coward
before I ever saw their courage.

They whispered:

Don't trust your own reflection.
and we listened
'cause the mirror was cracked.

They made our skin
a border.
A passport denied.
A reason to judge
the very face
we share.

They sent their lies across oceans
like warships,
like bibles,
like bullets,
aimed at the bond we never got to build.

But here's the quiet truth
they never meant for us to hear:

No one fights against a people
they believe are powerless.
No one fears the unity
they don't see coming.

The disdain was planted.
Watered with shame.
Harvested in confusion.

And still ~

We recognize each other.
In the drumbeat.
In the accents carried by wind.
In the silence where our ancestors shout
Remember.

We are not enemies.
We are evidence.
That survival runs deeper
than propaganda.

That Black
is a global language,
spoken through wounds
that are still
healing.

The lie is the barrier.
The truth is the reunion.
And the truth?
Is rising.

We Shine Anyway

They wear the mask of judgment
when they look at us,
but beneath it,
there's a flicker ~
a recognition they can't control.

We are the branch that broke
yet still grew leaves.
The child stolen
who became a nation.
We built joy from ashes,
turned sorrow into a soundtrack
the whole world dances to.

They say we have no roots ~
but they speak our slang
without knowing our struggle.
They reject our culture
while wearing it like jewelry.

Somewhere inside that contradiction
is envy wearing colonial perfume.

Because we faced the monster
in its own lair
and didn't bow.
Because we carved a throne
out of trauma
and dared to sit on it
like royalty reborn.

We are not perfect ~
but we are undeniable.

They whisper *"you are not African,"*

because they feel the pressure
of a legacy they never had to rebuild.

We are the mirror
that reflects what was stolen
yet never fully erased.

And sometimes,
the brilliance of survival
burns the eyes of those
who were taught to see Blackness
only when it is humbled.

But listen ~

We do not shrink
for the comfort of the colonized.
We do not dim
for those still learning their shine.
We are the thunder
that announces liberation.
We are the beat
that refuses to surrender.

They may misunderstand us,
fear us,
envy us ~

But they cannot erase us.

We shine anyway.
We rise anyway.
We lead anyway.
We love anyway.

We are the children of stolen stars ~

and even in a foreign sky,
we learned
how to light up the night.

Saltwater Reunion

A Poem in Two Voices

AFRICA:
Ma chile, I know dat salt on ya tongue.
Dat sea breeze in ya chest.
Ya walk wide like de river still partin' fo' ya feet.
I been hearin' ya drum call
cross de Atlantic night.

GULLAH GEECHEE / BLACK AMERICA:
Mama, I been speakin' ya name
in de hush of Spanish moss,
in de shout of praise houses,
in rice fields where ghosts still sing
fo' freedom come true.

AFRICA:
Dey taught ya to fear me,
say I wuz witchcraft,
say Spirit be too loud in my bones.
But look ~
ya shout same as me,
ya cook same as me,
ya love same as me.

GULLAH GEECHEE:
Dey told me you forget me ~
dat I wuz sold away,
dat my roots drown in de water.
But Mama,
even de ocean couldn't wash you out my blood.

AFRICA:
I wuz cryin' when dey take you.
I wuz fightin' in every village,

every uprising dat neva make de books.
I wuz callin' ya back
in every liberation drum dat beat
fo' centuries.

GULLAH GEECHEE:
An I?
I wuz marchin' fo' all uh we.
Civil Rights in my backbone,
Harriet whisperin'
"Gwine home."
I wuz shoutin' "Free Africa!"
even when America ain't free me yet.

AFRICA:
Now look ~
you stand tall like baobab,
you carry sea and sovereignty
in ya spine.
You de child who survived
and still return.

GULLAH GEECHEE / BLACK AMERICA:
An you ~
you de mother who never stop prayin'
me home.

BOTH:
We two shores
'cross de same water.
Two names
fo' one people.
Saltwater kin
wid de same ancestors hummin'
in we bones.

Ain't no ship
ain't no gate
ain't no colonizer tongue
strong enough to break
what Spirit already bind.

We been one.
We still one.
We rise as one.

Candle for the Scammer

I am the author,
the one they tried to finesse
with a mystery number
and a cheap hustle in a borrowed suit.

They thought they found a victim,
but they summoned a witness ~
to my growth,
to my glow,
to my God-given authority.

I lit a candle…
Not for love,
not for light,
but for **GPS** ~
So their scam could find its way
back to where it came from.

May their WiFi buffer forever,
may their spam calls drop in deliverance,
may every "Congratulations!" text
get swallowed by the void
they crawled out of.

My ancestors took roll call and said:
"Who sent you?"
Then told me, calmly:
"Oh no baby, NOT this one."

So I rebuked the scam,
blocked the number,
and returned that dusty energy
to the sender
with express shipping
and no refunds.

Because I'm a published author,
not a pressed target.

Saints and scammers beware:
This ink is protected.
This phone is guarded.
This glow is spiritual and hood-certified.

I lit a candle for the scammer ~
but don't get it twisted…

We can light more.

We Ain't for Sale

(A Poem for St. Helena Island)

We been here
long 'fore golf courses dreamed of takin' root,
long 'fore gates dared divide
water from shore,
people from home,
ancestors from the land that still remembers their names.

This soil?
It carries hymns in every grain,
prayers sewn deep like okra and sweetgrass,
stories that don't bow to developers' greed
or signatures wrapped in promises
we ain't ask for.

We stayed.
Through tides of chains.
Through laws that said we ain't belong
in the land we built.
We stayed.
On purpose.

Now they come again ~
shiny shoes, smiling sharp,
tryin' to buy what can't be bought.
Tryin' to erase our footprints
and build over our bones.

But we ain't goin' quiet.
We done marched too far,
we done prayed too loud,
we done outlived every storm they sent.

Hear us:

We ain't leavin'.
We ain't breakin'.
We ain't for sale.

St. Helena gon' stay St. Helena ~
no greens, no gated walls,
just home.
Just family.
Just the unbroken heartbeat
of Gullah/Geechee freedom.

And if they try to change their vote,
we'll lift our voices higher ~
until the sea itself repeats us:

Protect what our ancestors paid for in blood.
Stand firm like the roots that hold this island upright.
Land don't move ~ but we do.

United.
Watchful.
Homebound.
And still not for sale.

Lowcountry Conjure Man

(for James Brown)

He stomp that foot ~
and the earth remember the sound
of our grandmamas' bare heels on Carolina clay.

He scream ~
and the spirit answer,
coming up through the floorboards,
electric and holy.

He say *"Get on up!"*
and our bones rise
like buried prayers
called back into the body.

A Gullah ring shout in a red suit,
a praise break in platform shoes ~
the drum is his heartbeat,
the sweat is his offering.

Every "HUH!"
is a door he kicks open
for every Black soul holding back their shine.

He sing love like a hunger,
he fight the devil with a groove.
Ain't no shame in this salvation ~
we dance ourselves free.

James Brown:
Lowcountry conjure man,
Charleston fire in his feet,
Africa glowing in his hips,
turning the stage into a rootworker's altar.

He lay hands without touching you ~
and yet you feel healed.
He give us back our name:
POWER.
He give us back our dignity:
PROUD.

He told the world
the magic we already knew ~

Our rhythm is a weapon.
Our joy is a spell.
Our soul?
Our soul is sacred.

Lowcountry Conjure & Soul Power

Where I come from, music is **more than sound** ~ it is spirit work. In the Gullah Geechee South, rhythm is a language, a prayer, a way to keep ourselves whole when the world tries to break us. Our ancestors carried **Africa** into this land through the drum, the stomp, the clap ~ and when the drum was taken away, we became the drum.

The **Ring Shout** was our first church here:
feet circling on dirt floors, hands beating time, voices calling the ancestors forward. That same movement and fire survived in the Black church praise break, in the juke joint groove, in the holler of blues and jazz ~ and later, in soul and funk.

James Brown was born right there in that current.
South Carolina roots. Georgia grit.
All that Lowcountry conjure running through his veins.

When he dances ~ the spirit moves.

When he screams ~ the ancestors answer.
When he says *"Get on up!"* ~ even the tired bones in us rise.

People call him the Godfather of Soul.
But I know him as a **conjure man**.
A rootworker in a red suit,
channeling Africa in every hip,
turning the stage into holy ground.

Some folks only hear the beat and see the sweat.
But I hear **affirmations, protection, permission**.

Permission to feel joy.
Permission to take up space.
Permission to be loud and fully alive.

When James Brown performs, I feel the same power my grandmothers carried in their quiet palms ~
that **hush magic** that keeps our people living, loving, and surviving.

This is why his music feels spiritual to me.
Why I claim him as part of my culture and my story.

Because his sound reminds me:

We are still here.
Our soul is still sacred.
And our spirit still knows how to shout itself free.

Ring Shout

A sacred African American tradition of worship that survived enslavement in the Lowcountry. Participants move in a circle while clapping, stomping, and calling out to Spirit. It is prayer through rhythm and motion ~ a form of spiritual resistance and community healing that predates the Black church but still lives within it.

Hoodoo

An African diasporic spiritual system rooted in the American South, especially among Gullah Geechee people. Hoodoo uses herbs, roots, ancestors, and the natural world for protection, healing, justice, and empowerment. It is not a religion ~ it is **Black folk magic**, passed down through families.

Gullah Geechee

A distinct cultural group of African-descended people living along the coastal regions of South Carolina, Georgia, North Carolina, and Florida. The Gullah Geechee preserve strong African traditions in language, foodways, spirituality, and community ~ making their culture one of the most African in the United States.

Crossfire Queen

They tossed me into the middle ~
a battlefield made of skin tones
and insecurities
I never signed up to fight.

White girls called me "pretty for a Black girl"
then spit the word *Nigger*
like they needed to remind me
I was never one of them.

Black girls looked at my shade
like it was a warning label ~
light must mean weak,
long hair must mean arrogant,
soft features must mean
"she thinks she's better."

They came at me
like my existence was provocation.

But what they didn't know
was that my ancestors
built their strength into my bones
long before I took my first breath.

I learned to hold my ground
with a smile they couldn't decode ~
not meekness,
not softness,
just a different kind of power.

I am made of
whispers in cotton fields
and shouts from church pews,
of hidden love

and secret harm,
stitched into one unstoppable woman.

Every insult aimed at me
was a history lesson ~
that I am the child
of a legacy so strong
the world still doesn't know
how to categorize it.

They tried to hurt me
because they couldn't define me.
They tried to break me
because they couldn't place me.
They tried to dim me
because they couldn't ignore me.

But I survived
every side-eye,
every stereotype,
every bad intention.

Now I wear confidence
like armor
and joy
like war paint.

I am not confused.
I am complete.

A crossfire girl
who became a queen ~
crowned by everything
that tried to destroy her.

Light Skin Don't Mean Light Work

They see the glow
and think I'm a night-light ~
soft, harmless,
easy to handle.

Baby, this complexion
came from chaos.

I'm the product
of somebody's secrets,
somebody's rebellion,
somebody's survival story
they tried to hide
behind my shade.

Don't let this undertone fool you ~
my ancestors swing sweet tea
and revolution
in the same cup.

Yes, I'm light.
But my spirit?
Heavy.
Armed.
Unapologetic.

They expect sugar,
but I serve truth ~
unfiltered, unbothered,
and with a side of
"you got me fucked up."

I am not docile.
I am not diluted.
I am not your soft-focus fantasy.

I am a whole storm
that learned to look like sunshine
just to get through the door.

Light skin don't mean light work.
It means I glow under pressure ~
and still hit harder
than your assumptions.

PYT at the Funeral

They said keep it quiet,
keep it holy,
keep it still ~
but my spirit don't move like that.

The air was heavy,
the kind that swallows sound,
so I gave it a heartbeat ~
pressed play,
and let Michael sing what I couldn't say.

Pretty Young Thing ~
and the room cracked open,
like the sky when it can't hold the rain.
Tears met laughter,
and for one wild moment,
the sorrow danced.

Some clutched pearls,
some smiled through the ache,
and I swear I felt him there ~
not in the casket,
but in the rhythm,
clapping on the offbeat,
grinning that big grin of his,
saying, "That's right, sis ~
bring me back in light."

So I did.
Because sometimes healing ain't quiet,
sometimes love sounds like
a record spinning through grief,
a body remembering joy,
and a song that refuses to die.

Graveside Prayer

I placed a rose in the earth,
and for a moment,
the world stood still.
The sky leaned closer,
the wind carried names
only the soul could hear.

The soil was cool,
ancient and patient ~
it did not take,
it received.

My hand trembled,
but my heart understood:
this is how we say thank you,
how we return love
to the place it was born.

I watched the dirt fall
softly over the wood,
and knew that endings
are just a language
the spirit learns to speak.

Love doesn't vanish,
it changes form ~
root to root,
heart to heart,
life to light.

For Mike

I took a piece of the earth that held you,
a handful of silence
still warm with your name.

They told me dirt was final ~
but in my palm,
it felt alive,
like you were still speaking
between the grains.

I couldn't leave all of you behind.
Some part of me needed
to keep the weight of where you rest,
to hold proof
that love doesn't end
just because breath does.

Now, when I touch it,
I feel your laughter in the wind again,
and my tears fall softer,
like rain feeding what remains.

You are still here,
rooted in me,
in the soil,
in everything that dares to bloom.

Riding Through Fear

The bus became a battlefield.
A scream split the air ~
violence too close,
safety too far.

I saw what I never wanted to see:
a man bleeding fear,
begging strangers for help
no one felt brave enough to give.

Not because we didn't care,
but because caring has consequences
when danger knows your name,
your face,
your stop.

Evening rides feel like gambling ~
a ticket paid in tension,
eyes quietly scanning the exits,
heart rehearsing escape routes.

Mind alert.
Body tight.
Prayers whispered like seatbelt clicks.

We all want to go home.
We all want to believe
that public transit is a public good
and not a rolling reminder
how fragile peace can be.

Yet here I am,
still climbing aboard ~
bravery disguised as routine.
Hoping the next ride

feels like this one…
quiet, sunlit, ordinary.

And if fear rides with me,
so does resilience.
I am not the violence I've witnessed ~
I am the courage that keeps moving
despite it.

The Man Who Survived the Rivers

Born somewhere in Pennsylvania soil,
around 1820 ~ a time when men
were built from iron and absence,
when freedom was a word still fighting
to mean what it should.

He raised a family
in the shadow of Conemaugh's waters,
carving a life out of mountains and steel,
working days that bent his back
but couldn't break his name.

He loved a woman named Irena ~
buried her too soon,
left with children who needed
his voice, his hands,
his stubborn hope.

I imagine him tired
but still rising before the sun,
still showing up
even when the world asked too much
and gave too little.

In 1878, the river town took him back ~
laid him in the earth he worked,
a quiet burial
for a loud legacy.

And now here I am ~
blood of his blood,
spirit of his survival ~
writing him back into memory.

I carry the grit

he never got to name,
the dreams he never had time to chase,
the story that refused
to stay buried.

I am proof
that he lived,
that he loved,
that he mattered ~
and that the river
did not wash him away.

The Rise: Healing, Pride & Self-Love

This section rises from the quiet places where hurt once lived. Here is where healing takes its first breath, where softness becomes strength, where boundaries become sacred, and where you return to yourself with power and grace.

STD

(Self Trauma Dismantling)

I've been infected
by the things I never asked for ~
old wounds passed down
like secrets no one wanted to name.

Trauma that clung to me
like a shadow on my skin,
a history written in my body
before I ever learned the words "heal."

But I'm not letting that pain
keep reproducing in me.
Not anymore.

I'm breaking cycles
like I break bad habits ~
slow, clumsy,
and still showing up.

I'm disinfecting the lies
that told me I was too much
and somehow not enough
at the same damn time.

I'm learning to breathe
without apologizing for it.
Learning that loving myself
is not an act of rebellion ~
it's medicine.

This new STD
comes with side effects:

freedom in the throat,
peace in the chest,
boundaries like locked doors
I no longer explain.

Every day,
I take another dose of truth,
a treatment plan of softness,
a ritual of saying,
"I deserve to be whole."

And I do.
I do.
I do.

I'm dismantling the trauma
that tried to settle in my bloodline ~
healing myself
so the next generation
won't have to.

This time,
I'm the cure.

The Way I Heal

I'm a Libra learning
that balance doesn't mean bending
until my backbone snaps.
Peace doesn't mean quieting my own storm
so someone else can sleep through theirs.

I'm a Pisces Moon
who feels every shift in the universe ~
who knew heartbreak
before I ever knew language for it.
I'm learning not to drown
in what isn't mine to carry.

I'm a Scorpio Rising
with a history that refuses to stay silent.
Transformation sits on my tongue
like a prayer and a warning ~
I have died to become myself
more times than anybody knows.

So here's how I heal now:

I choose me
even when they call it selfish.
I let go
even when my hands are shaking.
I feel everything
but I don't let everything own me.

My softness is sacred.
My boundaries are holy.
My intuition is a map
that never leads me wrong.

I forgive myself

for the days I go quiet.
I honor the nights
my tears wash old ghosts away.
I celebrate every version of me
that kept living
when quitting felt easier.

I am the lover,
the dreamer,
the phoenix.

I rise beautifully,
I break gracefully,
I love fearlessly ~
and I always return
to myself.

I Call My Spirit Back from the Boo Hag
(An Invocation for My 52nd Year in Da Nang)

I wake with my legs dancing thunder,
my throat still echoing the dream scream ~
and I know who you are.
You, who ride the ones born with sight,
who test the blood of those marked by moonlight and memory.

You crossed the sea to find me again,
from the mossed porches of Charleston
to these soft rivers of Da Nang.
You know my scent ~ salt, sage,
and the hum of restless ancestors.
You know I am both island and tide.

But hear me now:
I am not a bed for your burden.
I am not a vessel for your unrest.
I am the granddaughter of root workers,
the daughter of prayer cloths and Psalms,
the keeper of lights that never go out.

If you come to warn me ~
speak plain.
If you come to guide me ~
step gentle.
If you come to ride me ~
know this: I ride back.

My bones remember the language of protection.
My skin remembers the saltwater path home.
My spirit is no longer afraid of mirrors or midnight.

So I breathe your name out

and call my own back in:
I am here. I am whole. I am unclaimed by fear.
You may walk with me in peace,
but you will not take my rest again.

Morning Bus Peace

Today the bus forgot its chaos,
left the noise at the stop
with the rushing and the rudeness
that usually boards with me.

Sunlight spilled into the seats
like it finally found room to breathe,
while trees waved slow hellos
through clear windows ~
not smudged by the world's hurry.

I choose the quiet today.
I choose this open space
where my thoughts can sit beside me
instead of standing in the aisle
begging to be heard.

Here, I can feel myself ~
soft, unbothered, unpushed.
A whole sky riding with me
for the price of a fare.

Peace snuck in
with the morning air,
and for once,
I didn't miss it.

Between the Lines (West Liberty Avenue)

I love the idea of leaving.
The promise of elsewhere has always known my name.
My mother called it wanderlust ~
a hunger for horizons,
for air that feels different in the lungs.

But cars
hold memory.

I remember slick ice
and a street that forgot how to hold us.
The spin.
The sudden reversal.
The way oncoming traffic looked like fate
deciding whether to claim us.

West Liberty Avenue.
My body learned that name
before it learned the word fear.

Years later, I learned my cousin Eddie
would die on that same stretch of road ~
metal and fire,
no second chance.
Some roads do not forget the blood they take.

Now, when I am inside a car,
my body folds inward.
Claustrophobia presses its palms against my chest.
There is nowhere to run
and every sound feels final.

Traffic becomes a cage.
Cars flank me like walls.
The freeway closes its mouth.

I look down.
I write.
I breathe like breath is a contract with God.
I pray for safety
on my comings and goings
because I know how quickly
going can become gone.

I have driven before.
I know the rules of the road.
But knowledge does not erase memory,
and courage does not cancel survival.

Sometimes my body wants to open the door and flee ~
not because I want to die,
but because I want to live.

They call this anxiety.
They call it fear.
I call it a body
that remembers danger
and refuses to lie about it.

Still ~
I love travel.
I love movement.
I love the idea of arrival.

So I move carefully now.
With prayer tucked into my breath.
With writing as a handhold.
With reverence for the roads that raised me
and the ones that broke my trust.

This is not weakness.

This is history living in the nervous system.
This is what survival sounds like
when it is quiet.

I am not afraid of the world.
I am afraid of forgetting
how precious it is
to still be here.

Author's Note

This poem is rooted in lived experience.
The places are real.
The fear is remembered.
The prayers are ongoing.

The Future: Vision, Empowerment & Joy

This section looks forward ~ toward the woman you are still becoming, toward the dreams unfolding before you, toward the joy you now claim without apology. These poems honor your evolution, your clarity, and the future your ancestors prayed you into.

We Been One

AFRICA:
I birthed you in drums and dust,
wrapped you in night-sky constellations.
Your first cries were sung in Kiswahili,
in Mende prayers,
in the hush of river spirits guarding your sleep.

BLACK AMERICA:
And I carried those songs through ships and shadows,
through waters that tried to rename me silence.
I braided your memory into my backbone,
so even when they broke me,
I still stood like a hymn.

AFRICA:
They told me you were lost ~
that the ocean devoured your name.
So I learned to miss children
I had no funeral for.
I became a mother with one arm reaching toward the sea.

BLACK AMERICA:
They told me you abandoned me ~
that you sold me for salt and guns.
So I learned to survive
without a map to where my bones began.

AFRICA:
But look ~
your spirit still speaks Twi in its sleep,
Still dances like the ancestors are whispering "again!"
You are my wandering star.
A warrior baptized in fire.

BLACK AMERICA:

And look ~
your courage walks through Harlem,
and Selma, and Watts,
your heartbeat is the beat of my drums ~
I was never cut off, only replanted.

AFRICA:
Child, I never forgot you.

BLACK AMERICA:
Mama, I never let you go.

BOTH:
Let them divide us
so they can collect our diamonds
and crucify our freedom
no more.

We are two halves of the same unbroken soul ~
continent and diaspora,
ancestor and descendant,
drum and echo.

We have always known each other.
We have always been each other.

We been one.
We are one.
We will rise as one.

Royal Remix

I am not a fraction.
I am not a question mark.
I am not a diluted version
of anything sacred.

I am the remix of royalty ~
the drumline of West Africa
still beating beneath my skin,
the rice fields of the coast
still whispering my name.

My bloodline didn't ask permission
to survive history ~
it just did.

Kidnapped nations in my DNA,
but not one drop defeated.
Africa didn't disappear ~
it multiplied in me.

I am kingdoms that crossed the ocean,
palaces reforged in the fire,
languages reborn in a new land,
ancestors who refused extinction
so I could open my mouth
and say:
I am still here.

Call me complicated if you must ~
that's just another word
for too much greatness to simplify.

I am the child of salted shores
and rebel futures,
of memory that outlived the chains.

I am Africa
twice over ~
once by origin
again by resilience.

Crown not required ~
my existence is the inheritance.

Both Black & Unbothered

They love to tell me what a Black person should believe ~
like freedom comes with a checklist,
or liberation is locked behind one political door.

But I am my own permission.

I am pro-Black ~
the kind that remembers family is a revolution,
and stability is a form of protest.
I believe in fathers who stay,
mothers who lead,
children who rise on solid ground.

I believe in our legacy
and the roots that hold us upright.

They call me conservative
like it's a contradiction ~
but my values are older than their labels.
Black love is ancient.
Black tradition is sacred.
We built our survival on faith, stewardship,
wisdom passed from porch to pew
and from struggle to Sunday dinner.

I don't trust any system
that profits from our pain
or celebrates when we fall apart.
I question anything that claims to help us
but feeds on our wounds.
If that makes me different,
then different is divine.

I want our people thriving ~
not just alive.

I want marriages unbroken,
villages restored,
boys grown into men
who know their worth
and girls crowned with dignity
that never cracks.

So no ~ I am not confused.
I am not a contradiction.
I am a reminder.

We can love our Blackness
and love our structure.
We can fight for our culture
and fight for our families.
We can break every box
and still honor the blueprint
our ancestors drew in the dirt
with their own blood.

I am both.
Boldly.
Unapologetically.
Black in every breath ~
and committed to the strength
that keeps us standing.

If they don't understand,
tell them this:

I'm not choosing sides.
I'm choosing us.

A Letter to My First Grandbaby

Before I held you,
I imagined you.

I wondered whose eyes you would carry,
whose laugh would slip out when you were not looking,
which ancestor would recognize you first.

This book was written before you arrived,
but not before you were present.
You were already part of the future
I was writing toward.

One day, if you find these pages,
I hope you feel surrounded.
Not instructed~
but held.

Know this:
You come from people who survived,
people who prayed,
people who loved loudly and quietly at the same time.
You come from roots that go deep
and branches that refuse to stop reaching.

I may not always have the right words,
but I will always have room for you.

With all of me,
Grandma

Acknowledgments

This book was shaped by memory, conversation, silence, and survival. I offer my gratitude to the women whose lives and stories ~ spoken and unspoken ~ made this work possible. To the ancestors who carried what could not be named, and to the living who continue the work of remembering, thank you.

I am grateful to my family for their presence, their endurance, and their love across generations. To every reader who recognizes themselves in these pages, may you feel seen, held, and affirmed.

About the Author

Emily Clarida is a writer whose work explores ancestry, identity, healing, and self-return through poetry and prose. Rooted in Southern, Gullah Geechee, and spiritual traditions, her writing bridges memory and lived experience, honoring the past while making space for wholeness in the present.

Her work centers the voices of women, the weight of inherited history, and the quiet power of resilience. All of Me: *Light Work, Heavy History* reflects her ongoing commitment to truth-telling, remembrance, and transformation.

Ritual Sound

These poems were written to rhythm ~
to basslines that carried memory,
to drumbeats that held both grief and power.

If you'd like to enter the soundscape that shaped this work,
listen to the James Brown Hoodoo Playlist:

Permissions & Credits

All text in this book is the original work of the author. Photographs and visual materials are either original to the author, used with permission, or believed to be in the public domain.

Every effort has been made to identify and credit sources appropriately.

Connect with the Author

Website: www.emilyclarida.com

Instagram: @emilyclaridawrites

TikTok: @emilyclaridawrites

Email: emilyclarida.author@gmail.com

The story does not end here.

It continues in the blood,

in the breath,

in the becoming.

—

All of Me

Coming 2026

All My Names: Harmon – Davis Legacy

www.ingramcontent.com/pod-product-compliance
Lightning Source LLC
LaVergne TN
LVHW041609070526
838199LV00052B/3051